The Ultimate Sleepover Guide

by Gaia Merriman

SCHOLASTIC INC.

Table of Contents

Ready, Set, Sleepover!

Having a slumber party with one (or more!) of your BFFs is the perfect way to build the bestie bond. Are you ready for a night of friendship and fun? Then you've come to the right place! Inside this book you'll find tips for throwing the ultimate sleepover, as well as awesome activities, quizzes, and recipes to keep you and your friends giggling and gabbing all night long!

You're invited . . .

There are lots of unique and fun ways to send out slumber party invitations. Here are a few ideas to get you started!

★ Love communicating with your pals via text and email? Why not send out a slumber party e-vite? There are lots of free websites where you can choose a pre-made invitation to personalize with your party details. Ask an adult to help you find a good website and enter the emails of your friends or their parents. Then sit back and wait for the RSVPs to roll in!

★ Are you and your friends known for your frequent note passing? If so, a snail mail invitation might be just the thing! You can make and mail out fun invitations with pictures of sleeping bags, pajamas, or even cute cupcakes on them.

★ Do you and your BFFs love to be one-of-a-kind? Do a surprise hand-delivery of your invitations to each guest! If you want to take your originality one step further, tuck each invitation inside a pair of slippers or decorate and write the party details on plain pillowcases!

You're Invited to a
Sleepover

You're Invited!

The 5 Ws

Now that you have the perfect invitation design, it's time to let your guests know the details! Not sure what information to include? A great place to start is with the Who, What, When, Where, and Why of the occasion!

Who is throwing the party? (That's you!)

_____

What do your guests need to bring? (Sleeping bag, pillow, toothbrush, PJs, anything special they will need for the party)

_____

When will the party begin and end?

_____

Where will the party take place? (Make sure to write your address.)

_____

Why are you having the party? Is it a birthday or special occasion?

_____

Make sure you include a telephone number or email address for RSVPs so you know how many friends are coming!

Party Packing 101

Never forget any slumber party essentials with this ultimate overnight checklist!

- ✓ Sleeping bag
- ✓ Pillow
- ✓ Pajamas
- ✓ Slippers
- ✓ A change of clothes
- ✓ Hairbrush
- ✓ Toothbrush
- ✓ Toothpaste
- ✓ Swimsuit and towel if there will be water activities

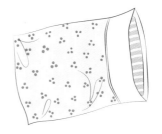

brite

What's Your Sleepover Style?

Do you want your sleepover to be as unique as you and your friends are
Then take the quiz below to find your perfect sleepover party theme!

What's your ideal vacation destination?

A. The Grand Canyon

B. New York City

C. Canada

D. Miami

It's movie night! What's your top pick?

A. An adventure like *Homeward Bound*

B. A classic like *Breakfast at Tiffany's*

C. A funny favorite like *Finding Nemo*

D. A Cinderella story like *The Princess Diaries*

Breakfast is nutritious AND delicious, so what does your morning meal look like?

A. Scrambled eggs and toast

B. Waffles with strawberries and whipped cream

C. A bowl of cereal

D. Yogurt-and-granola parfait

What type of music gets you grooving when you're in the car?

A. Country music

B. Pop music

C. Rock 'n' roll music

D. Calming instrumental music

Your room is in need of a makeover! What color do you decide to paint the walls?

A. Green

B. Purple

C. A different color for each wall

D. Pink

What's your first-day-of-school fashion go-to?

A. Something easy and comfortable like jeans and a T-shirt

B. You check out what your favorite celebrities are wearing and use it as inspiration for a trendy look

C. Neon all the way—you're not ready for the summer to end!

D. Yoga pants and a T-shirt with a positive message printed on the front

You scream, I scream, we all scream for ice cream! What's your favorite flavor?

A. Rocky Road

B. Strawberry

C. Mint Chocolate Chip

D. Vanilla

The weekend is finally **here,** and you and your friends have plans to hang out! What do you decide to spend the day doing?

A. Go to a park and play soccer or kickball

B. Head to a pool or go window-shopping

C. Hit the bowling lanes or a mini golf course

D. Paint your nails and try out new hairstyles on one another

You're a girl of many talents, but what's your dream job?

A. Forest ranger

B. Actress

C. Airline pilot

D. Chef

If you could pick one animal to be your Spirit Animal, what would it be?

A. Bear

B. Cat

C. Bird

D. Horse

Your Sleepover Style Score

Mostly A's = Camping Slumber Party

- Create invitations shaped like flashlights.

- Build blanket forts for indoor camping or set up tents in the yard for sleeping under the stars.

- Make s'mores or have a cookout.

Mostly B's = Hollywood Glam Slumber Party

- Send out invitations designed like movie tickets.
- Create a DIY popcorn station with creative toppings like candy or caramel sauce.
- Hang a large white sheet on a wall and set up a projector to create a big screen for your favorite flick!

Mostly C's = Glow-in-the-Dark Slumber Party

- Write your invitations in glow-in-the-dark marker so your guests have to read it in the dark.
- Buy glow sticks from the dollar store to make bracelets, necklaces, or glow crowns.
- Create a starry glow-in-the-dark night sky on your ceiling for you and your friends to sleep under.

Mostly D's = Spa Slumber Party

- Include a mini nail polish with each invitation.
- Make your own spa treatments like the chocolate face mask on page 25!
- Set up DIY manicure and pedicure stations with a variety of nail polish colors, cotton swabs, nail polish remover, and an inspiration board of nail design ideas.

Top 10 Slumber Party Movies

A top sleepover activity once the sun goes down is watching a great movie! If you're not sure which flick to pick, take a look at the list below for ideas. What's the one thing these movies all have in common? Great friendships, of course!

The Parent Trap

Harry Potter and the Sorcerer's Stone

The Goonies

Dolphin Tale

The Princess Diaries

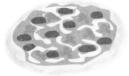

Mary Poppins

The Wizard of Oz

Toy Story

Annie

Akeelah and the Bee

Recipe Roundup

Are you and your besties budding chefs? Get creative in the kitchen at your next sleepover with these fun and delicious recipes!

No-Bake Mini Pizza Party

Prep Time: 10 Minutes   Total Time: 10 Minutes

What You'll Need
- Pre-cooked biscuits OR English muffins
- Pizza sauce or pesto
- Shredded mozzarella cheese (or mix it up and try cheddar, feta, or even goat cheese)
- Toppings! Topping ideas: pepperoni, peppers, olives, mushrooms, or even pineapple

Preparation
1. Provide each guest with two biscuit or English muffin halves (or maybe one of each). Let each guest personalize her "pizza crust" with the sauce, toppings, and cheese of her choice.
2. Enjoy pizza cold or microwave for 25 seconds until the cheese is melted.

No-Bake Fruit "Pizza"

Prep Time: 10 Minutes   Total Time: 10 Minutes

What You'll Need

- "Crust" ideas: Whole-grain tortilla, pita bread, flat bread
- "Sauce" ideas: peanut butter or another nut butter, cream cheese, Greek yogurt, jam, hazelnut spread
- Topping ideas: apples, bananas, kiwis, berries, grapes, raisins, cranberries, coconut flakes, sliced almonds, granola, mini chocolate chips

Preparation

1. Give each guest a "crust" to spread with one (or more!) types of "sauce."
2. Have each person add toppings and then cut the pizza into wedges, fold it like a quesadilla, or roll it up like a burrito!

Be sure to ask your guests if they have any food allergies or restrictions before you start cooking. It's more fun if everyone can join in!

Crazy for Cocoa Chocolate Disks

Prep Time: 10 Minutes   Cook Time: 60 Minutes
Total Time: 1 Hour 10 Minutes

What You'll Need

- 1/2 cup coconut oil
- 1/2 cup cocoa powder
- 3 tablespoons honey
- 1/2 teaspoon vanilla extract
- Mix-in ideas: chopped nuts, coconut flakes, sea salt, candy, peanut butter, orange zest, cinnamon

Preparation

1. Let the coconut oil sit at room temperature or microwave for 5-10 seconds until it becomes liquefied.
2. Mix together coconut oil, cocoa powder, honey, and vanilla extract until well blended.
3. Prepare a muffin tin with paper liners and fill each cup 1/4 of the way full.
4. Add desired mix-ins to each chocolate disk. Freeze chocolates for 1 hour, then peel away the wrapper and enjoy!

*Note: Chocolate must be kept refrigerated

Sleepover S'mores

Prep Time: 5 Minutes   Cook Time: 2 Minutes
Total Time: 7 Minutes

What You'll Need

- Microwave-safe plate
- Ripe bananas
- Chocolate chips
- Mini marshmallows
- Crushed graham crackers
- Topping ideas: chopped nuts, rainbow sprinkles, whipped cream, granola, your favorite cereal, chocolate syrup, hazelnut spread

Preparation

1. Cut bananas down the center vertically and fill with chocolate chips and marshmallows. Place bananas on a microwave-safe plate and microwave for 1-2 minutes or until the filling has melted and the bananas are slightly softened.

2. Remove from microwave and sprinkle with graham cracker crumbles and any additional toppings!

Party-Perfect Parfait

Do you and your BFFs love to try new things? Parfaits are creamy, delicious desserts that you create by layering together a base, fruit, and flavor. Take your taste buds on an adventure and create your signature dessert!

Prep Time: 5 Minutes   Total Time: 5 Minutes

Preparation

1. Use the chart on the next page to design your perfect dessert parfait.
2. Put 1/4 cup of your base at the bottom of the cup.
3. Add a thin layer of fruit on top of your base, followed by your flavor choice.
4. Now repeat the layering process: Add another 1/4 cup of your base and follow with your fruit and flavor choices.
5. Top off your parfait with 2-3 spoonfuls of your base (just enough to cover your last flavor addition

Dig In and enjoy!

Parfait
DIY Chart

Base - Pick 1

Yogurt
Greek yogurt
Frozen yogurt
Ice cream
Sorbet

Fruit - Pick 1-2

Bananas
Strawberries
Apples
Blueberries
Mango
Blackberries
Peaches
Raspberries
Pineapple
Raisins

Flavor - Pick 1-2

Granola
Cinnamon
Vanilla extract
Caramel sauce
Hazelnut spread
Maple syrup
Honey
Mint
Chopped nuts
Whipped cream

This or That?
Food Edition!

Are you and your bestie known for always liking the same things, or are you as opposite as opposite can be? Take turns asking and answering the questions in this quiz to see how your food favorites compare!

? ○ **Hot Chocolate or OJ?** ○

○ Pizza or Popcorn? ○

○ **Sweet or Salty?** ○ ?

○ Hamburgers or Hot Dogs? ○

○ **Chocolate or Vanilla?** ○

? ○ Cookies or Cupcakes? ○

○ **Breakfast or Lunch?** ○ ?

○ Corn Chips or Potato Chips? ○

○ **Carrots or Cucumbers?** ○

○ String Cheese or Cheese Crackers? ○

○ **Cake or Ice Cream?** ○

? ○ Apples or Bananas? ○

○ **Peanut Butter or Almond Butter?** ○ ?

○ Waffles or Pancakes? ○

○ **Ravioli or Spaghetti?** ○

○ Pesto or Tomato Sauce? ○

What's Your Vacation Style?

Are you and your best friend twin-tastic travelers? Take turns completing the quiz below and then compare your results to find out how closely your perfect getaways align!

What's your ideal way of traveling to your vacation destination?

A. By plane

B. By boat

C. By car

D. By train

What is the one thing you never leave the house without when you travel?

A. Your pillow

B. Your MP3 player

C. Your journal

D. Your camera

It's your birthday, and you get to spend the day doing whatever you'd like. What do you decide to do?

A. Go to a spa and get your nails done

B. Go to a water park

C. Go window-shopping and out to a restaurant

D. Go to a museum

You're packing your carry-on bag and toss in something to read on the trip. What type of reading material are you most likely to bring?

A. A magazine

B. A crossword or puzzle book

C. A travel guidebook

D. A historical novel

You decide to treat yourself to a manicure while on vacation! What color do you choose?

A. Aqua

B. A clear polish

C. A French manicure

D. Red

You're in NYC, but only for one day. What do you decide to do?

A. Book it to Brooklyn for a picnic in the park

B. Go out to dinner and see a Broadway show

C. Visit the Empire State Building and Times Square

D. Take the train to Coney Island for a roller-coaster ride and a stroll on the boardwalk

Your Vacation Style Score

Mostly A's = Rest and Relaxation

Whether it's a manicure or a day by the pool, you love to spend your vacation getting pampered. Warm and tropical locations like Florida or the Caribbean have the calm, relaxing vibe that matches your vacation mood!

Mostly B's = All-the-Time Action

You love to fill your vacation days with all different types of activities. You're always up for hot or cold weather, just as long as you can spend time outdoors snowboarding, swimming, or biking!

Mostly C's = City Sightseeing

Your ideal vacation destination is a city. Whether it's climbing to the top of the tallest building or getting pizza from a famous local shop, there's nothing you love more than visiting all the highlights that a new place has to offer!

Mostly D's = Blast to the Past

You're a complete history buff who loves learning the stories behind old buildings or statues you come across on your travels. You like to spend your vacation days wandering through museums or visiting historical sights!

Sleepover Spa Soirée

Ready for some relaxation? Raid the kitchen to create a head-to-toe home spa experience for you and your friends!

Flavored Lip Gloss

Keep your lips shiny and moist with this easy at-home lip gloss! Try out a classic flavored drink mix like cherry, or get crazy and go for a pink lemonade— or tropical punch—flavored gloss.

What You'll Need

- 2 tablespoons coconut oil
- 1/2 package flavored drink mix
- Enough water to form a paste
- 1 teaspoon sugar
- Small containers to store lip gloss

Directions

1. Microwave the coconut oil for 5 seconds or until it is soft but not completely liquefied.
2. In a separate cup, pour in half of the drink mix package and add just enough water to form a paste and see the color.
3. Mix in the sugar and add coconut oil a little at a time until the paste i the desired color. Stir until sugar is dissolved and paste is smooth.
4. Spoon the gloss into small containers and refrigerate briefly before enjoying!

Good-Enough-to-Eat Chocolate Face Mask

This decadent face mask will moisturize your skin, leaving it feeling smooth and silky. Best of all, it's totally edible!

What You'll Need
- 1/3 cup cocoa powder
- 3 tablespoons heavy cream
- 2 teaspoons cottage cheese
- 1/4 cup honey
- 3 teaspoons oatmeal

Directions
1. Combine all ingredients and stir until well mixed.
2. Smear a generous layer onto your face and relax for 10 minutes before rinsing off with warm water.

Easy-As-Apple-Pie Skin Polish

Get rid of dead skin cells and dirt on the surface of your skin with this divine apple exfoliant. Added bonus: You'll smell as sweet as pie all day long!

What You'll Need
- 2 tablespoons brown sugar
- 2 tablespoons granulated sugar
- 1 tablespoon applesauce
- 1/8 teaspoon cinnamon

Directions
1. Mix together all ingredients.
2. If you plan to use the scrub on your face, leave out granulated sugar from the recipe as it is too rough for your skin.
3. Then, in a bath or shower, apply the scrub to your skin using a washcloth or sponge.
4. Rinse well and moisturize with body lotion.

Sweet-As-Honey Oatmeal Yogurt Mask

eep your skin looking smooth and clear with this gentle, natural skin
eanser.

What You'll Need
- 1/4 cup plain yogurt or buttermilk
- 1/2 cup oatmeal
- 2 tablespoons honey

Directions
1. Finely grind oatmeal in a blender and set aside.
2. In a separate bowl, combine honey and yogurt.
3. Add oatmeal and mix together until a smooth paste forms.
4. Apply to your face and neck and leave on for 15 minutes
   before rinsing with warm water.

Cool-As-a-Cucumber Eye Soother

Take care of irritated and puffy eyes after a long night of fun and games at your sleepover with this quick fix! Cucumbers are full of vitamin C and caffeic acid, both of which help reduce swelling. You and your besties will be looking cool, calm, and collected in no time!

What You'll Need

- Cucumber
- Ice
- Washcloth

Directions
1. Cut the cucumber into 1/2-inch-thick slices and place over ice to chill.
2. Once cool, put a slice over each eye and cover with a warm washcloth.
3. Sit back and relax for 10–15 minutes before removing the slices.

Strawberry Hand Spa

Get your hands manicure-ready with this sweet strawberry exfoliant. Strawberries contain a natural fruit acid that helps the exfoliating process!

What You'll Need

- 8–10 strawberries
- 2 tablespoons of apricot oil or olive oil
- 1 teaspoon of coarse salt such as sea salt

Directions

1. Combine all ingredients and mash into a paste.
2. Massage the paste onto your hands, then rinse and dry.
3. Apply lotion for added moisture once you're finished.

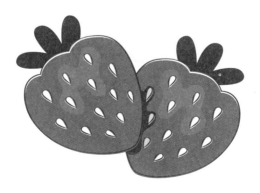

Milk Foot Spa

Start your pedicure off right with a treat for the feet! Soak them in this milk-and-water bath, followed by a sugar scrub. Your feet will be silky smooth and pedi ready!

What You'll Need
- 7 cups water
- 2 cups milk
- 1/2 cup sugar
- 2 tablespoons lotion

Directions
1. Mix together the water and milk, and heat until the mixture is lukewarm.
2. Put milk mixture in a container large enough to fit your feet. Soak feet for 10–15 minutes.
3. Combine sugar and lotion. Massage the mixture onto your feet to exfoliate.
4. Rinse with warm water and dry. Apply additional lotion to feet as needed or desired!

Nail Art Salon

Set up an at-home salon and let your inner artist shine! You and your friends can take turns giving one another manis and pedis. Create picture-perfect nails with the tutorials below, then experiment and come up with your own designs!

Polka-Dot Perfect French Manicure

What You'll Need

- Dotting tool such as a pointed cotton swab, bobby pin, toothpick, or unfolded paper clip
- Neutral polish color such as white or nude for the base coat
- Variety of bright-colored polishes for the polka-dot French tips
- Clear top coat polish

Step 1: Paint each nail with your neutral polish. A light base coat will allow your polka dots to really stand out and shine!

Step 2: Dab a small dot of polish on top of your cotton swab or dotting tool and put evenly spaced dots across the tip of each nail. Use a different color of polish for the dots on each fingernail or keep it simple with just one!

Step 3: Let your dots dry completely before adding a top coat to avoid any smearing.

Flower Power Pedicure

Now that you've perfected the polka dot, use your skills to create fancy flower designs!

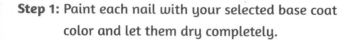

What You'll Need
- Dotting tool such as a pointed cotton swab, bobby pin, toothpick, or unfolded paper clip
- Base coat color of your choice
- Flower petal polish color of your choice
- Clear top coat polish

Step 1: Paint each nail with your selected base coat color and let them dry completely.

Step 2: Select the polish for your flower color and use your dotting tool to create five dots in a circle. Let sit for 45 seconds and then plac[e] a toothpick in the center of each dot and lightly drag it to the center of the circle to transform your dots into petals!

Step 3: Let your dots dry completely before adding a top coat to avoid any smearing.

PRO TIP: Dry nails faster by filling a container with ice water and submerging your nails for three minutes

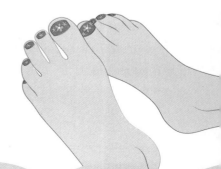

Blindfold Makeover Game

you and your friends are ready to LOL all night, this game is for you.
ll you need is a blindfold, some makeup, and a few friends who are
ady for a new look! Eye shadow, blush, and lipstick are all great for
is game, but avoid mascara as it could get in the eyes.

Step 1: Put a number in a hat for each person who will be getting a makeover and have everyone select one. This is the order in which you will give your makeovers!

Step 2: Person #1 puts on the blindfold and applies makeup to person #2. Person #2 will then do the same for person #3 and so on until everyone has had a turn. The last person to go can make over person #1.

Step 3: Take pictures of each makeover so you have the memories!

Ultimate Slumber Party DIYs

Let your creativity shine with these awesome do-it-yourself projects to share with your BFFs!

Classic Chinese Staircase Friendship Bracelet

Difficulty Level: Easy

Materials
- 1 color of embroidery floss
- Scissors
- Tape

Instructions

Step 1:
Cut three 40-inch-long pieces of thread and one 70-inch-long piece of thread and tie them together. Leave at least a 1-inch tail.

Step 2:
Tape the tail of your string to a flat surface and spread out your string in this pattern: 1, 2, 3, 4. String 1 should be the 70-inch-long string.

Step 3:

Take string I and knot it around all other strings. Pull tightly until your knot slides to the top of the bracelet. Repeat this knotting step using string I until your bracelet is big enough to fit around your wrist! As the spiral pattern appears, reposition your bracelet so your knotting is always in front of you.

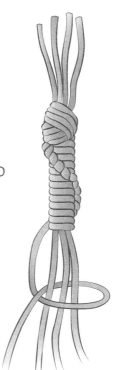

Step 4:

When you reach the desired length, tie the strings together, leaving at least a I-inch tail. You can tie the two ends together to make a bracelet fit for a BFF!

Deluxe Diagonal Friendship Bracelet

Difficulty Level: Medium

Materials
- 4 different colors of embroidery floss
- Scissors
- Tape

> 1 = your first color
> 2 = your second color
> 3 = your third color
> 4 = your fourth color

Instructions

Step 1:
Begin with 40 inches of each color thread and tie them together. Leave at least a 1-inch tail.

Step 2:
Tape the tail of your string to a flat surface and spread out your string in this pattern: 1, 2, 3, 4.

Step 3:

Take string 1 in your left hand and string 2 in your right hand. Knot string 1 around string 2 and pull tightly until your knot slides to the top of the bracelet. Repeat with strings 1 and 2. Now do the same two knots with string 1 and string 3 and then string 1 and string 4.

Step 4:

String 2 will now be on the left end. Repeat Step 3 with strings 2, 3, and 4 and then start again with string 1. Continue until your bracelet is the right length. Tie a knot, again leaving at least a 1-inch tail, and you're done!

Difficulty Level: Hard

Materials

- 3 different colors of
    embroidery floss
- Scissors
- Tape

> I = your first color
> 2 = your second color
> 3 = your third color

Instructions

Step I:

Begin with 70 inches of each thread, fold them in half, and tie a loop.

I 2 3 3 2

Step 2:

Tape the loop of your string to a flat surface and spread out your string colors in this pattern: I, 2, 3, 3, 2, I.

Step 3:

Take string I from the left in your left hand, and strin 2 from the left in your right hand. Knot string I aroun string 2 and pull tightly until your knot slides to the top of the bracelet. Repeat with strings I and 2 creating two knots in total. Now do the same two knots with string I and string 3.

Step 4:

Repeat step 3 with strings 1, 2, and 3 on the right side. You should now have both strings 1's in the middle and both string 2's on the ends.

Step 5:

Tie the two string 1's in the middle together into a knot. Repeat and tie a second knot with the two string 1's.

Step 6:

Repeat steps 3, 4, and 5 with string 2 on the left and then right side. Repeat steps 3, 4, and 5 with string 3 on the left and then the right side. Now start with string 1 again. Continue repeating these steps with strings 1, 2, and 3 until your bracelet is the right length. Tie a knot at the end and share!

Sleep Sweet Dream Catcher

A dream catcher is something you create and hang by your bed to "catch" your bad dreams and only let through the good ones. Create your own dream catcher and get ready to have the best night's sleep of your life!

Materials

- Paper plate
- Scissors
- Hole Punch
- Paint
- Yarn
- Feathers
- Beads
- Stickers/markers/crayons/ colored pencils

Instructions

Step 1:

Cut a hole in the middle of your paper plate, leaving about 2 inches of rim. Punch 10 evenly spaced holes around the inside edge of the plate rim.

Step 2:

Color or decorate the rim of the plate. This will become your dream catcher base!

Step 3:

Randomly string your yarn through the holes bordering the plate. Add beads, feathers, or stickers for extra pizzazz!

Step 4:

Cut 5 pieces of yarn at random lengths and tie a feather to a knot at the bottom of each. Add beads above the feather and tie another knot.

Step 5:

Punch a new hole for each of the 5 strings on the bottom rim of your plate. Tie each string through a hole so they are dangling down like fringe. Hang your new dream catcher in your room and get ready for a night of sweet dreamin'!

What Kind of Friend Are You?
It's written in the stars . . .

Using your date of birth, find your Zodiac Sign below and read what it reveals about you as a friend!

Aries (March 21st–April 19th)

Aries are full of energy, like to stay busy, and enjoy a challenge. They are supportive and loyal friends who will do whatever it takes to lend a helping hand.
Zodiac Sign BFFs: Leo, Sagittarius, Aquarius, and Gemini

ARIES

Taurus (April 20th–May 20th)

Thoughtful and intelligent, Tauruses are known for being great advisers and leaders. Friends are as important as family to Tauruses, and they often have the same best friends for life!
Zodiac Sign BFFs: Capricorn, Cancer, Pisces, and Virgo

TAURUS

Gemini (May 21st–June 20th)

Geminis love to be social and try new things. Geminis are easy to talk to and are great listeners. They enjoy friendships that challenge them with new ideas.

Zodiac Sign BFFs: Aries, Leo, Libra, and Aquarius

GEMINI

Cancer (June 21st–July 22nd)

Cancers are sensitive and compassionate people who care deeply about their friends and family. Cancers can be shy when you first meet them, but they are supportive and loyal friends once you earn their trust.

Zodiac Sign BFFs: Taurus, Virgo, Scorpio, and Pisces

CANCER

Leo (July 23rd–August 22nd)

Leos are creative and independent people who love to be the center of attention. Leos enjoy being surrounded by friends and get along best with those who can keep up with their fast pace and high energy.

Zodiac Sign BFFs: Gemini, Libra, Aries, and Sagittarius

LEO

Virgo (August 23rd–September 22nd)

Virgos are hardworking, organized, and kind people who like to please others. They are easy to talk to and enjoy offering advice and helping friends solve problems.

Zodiac Sign BFFs: Cancer, Scorpio, Taurus, and Capricorn

VIRGO

Libra (September 23rd–October 22nd)

Libras are peaceful, cooperative, and social people who would rather be with friends than alone. Libras like things to be fair, and they work hard to resolve conflicts among their friends.

Zodiac Sign BFFs: Leo, Sagittarius, Gemini, and Aquarius

LIBRA

Scorpio (October 23rd–November 21st)

Scorpios are brave, determined, and wise people who make excellent leaders. They greatly value trust and honesty in friendships and may have a few close friends instead of many.

Zodiac Sign BFFs: Virgo, Capricorn, Cancer, and Pisces

SCORPIO

Sagittarius (November 22nd–December 21st)

Sagittarians are adventurous, open-minded, and always ready to travel. They love to laugh and make many new friends easily, especially those who share their love for adventure.

Zodiac Sign BFFs: Libra, Aquarius, Aries, and Leo

SAGITTARIUS

Capricorn (December 22nd–January 19th)

Capricorns are down-to-earth, responsible, and often serious people. They are caring and honest friends who are not afraid to offer their opinions and advice.

Zodiac Sign BFFs: Scorpio, Pisces, Taurus, and Virgo

CAPRICORN

Aquarius (January 20th–February 18th)

Aquarians are independent, unique, and optimistic people. They have many friends, but are very close to only a few people.

Zodiac Sign BFFs: Sagittarius, Aries, Gemini, and Libra

AQUARIUS

Pisces (February 19th–March 20th)

Pisces are artistic, generous, and forgiving. Pisces can tell when something is wrong, and they are known for helping their friends in need.

Zodiac Sign BFFs: Capricorn, Taurus, Cancer, and Scorpio

PISCES

A Handy Guide to Palm Reading

Palm reading, or palmistry, is a form of fortune-telling that has been around for thousands of years. Have you ever wished that you could see into the future? If so, this famous party trick is for you! Use the guide on the following pages to see what the future holds for you and your BFFs just by looking at your dominant (the one you write with) hand!

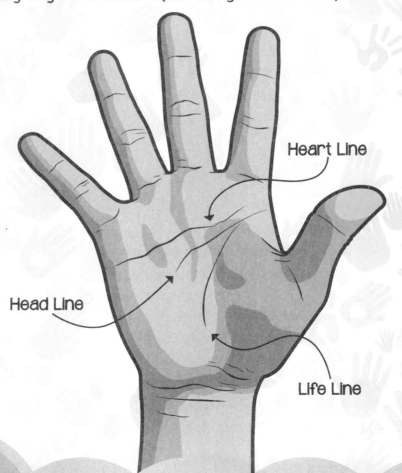

Heart Line

Head Line

Life Line

Head Line

The Head Line represents your mind and your smarts!

Short line:
You enjoy staying busy instead of having lots of quiet time.

Long line:
You take time to think things through before making decisions.

Curvy line:
You are creative and are always ready to have an adventure.

Straight line:
You are realistic and like to follow a schedule.

Wavy line:
You can be easily distracted.

Heart Line

The Heart Line represents your moods and emotions!

Short line:
You are independent and
enjoy your freedom.

Long, wavy line:
You are good at expressing
your feelings.

Curvy-all-over line:
You are friendly and like to
have people around.

Straight line:
You are down-to-earth and
consider others' feelings.

Life Line

The Life Line, sometimes called "the line of destiny," is all about your personality and major life events!

Long, deep line:
You are strong willed, confident, and like to stay active.

Short, shallow line:
You give your trust easily.

Wide, curvy line:
You have plenty of energy and enjoy being with others.

Close to your thumb:
You can get tired easily and enjoy quiet activities.

Break in the line:
You will have a major life change occur.

The True-Blue BFF Test

How strong is your bestie bond? Fill out one set of questions with the answers you think your friend will give and have your friend fill out the other set with the answers she thinks you will give. Then, take turns reading the questions and your answers aloud and see how well you an your best friend really know each other!

When is your friend's birthday? _____

What is your friend's favorite animal? _____

Does your friend have a secret talent? If so, what is it? _____

_____

What is one thing your friend is totally obsessed with? _____

_____

What is your friend's middle name? _____

Who is someone your friend admires? _____

What is your friend's favorite school subject? _____

If your friend could only eat one thing for the rest of her life,

what would it be? _____

What is your friend's favorite card or board game? _____

_____

Is your friend an ice cream cup or cone kind of girl? _____

When is your friend's birthday? _____

What is your friend's favorite animal? _____

Does your friend have a secret talent? If so, what is it? _____

_____

What is one thing your friend is totally obsessed with? _____

_____

What is your friend's middle name? _____

Who is someone your friend admires? _____

What is your friend's favorite school subject? _____

If your friend could only eat one thing for the rest of her life,

what would it be? _____

What is your friend's favorite card or board game? _____

_____

Is your friend an ice cream cup or cone kind of girl? _____

What Kind of Twins Are You and Your BFF?

You and your best friend have a special bond, but just how close are you? Take this quiz to see whether you're as tight as twins!

1. It's Saturday night and you and your BFF are having a sleepover! First order of business: ordering pizza. Which toppings do you decide on?

   a. You love peppers and your best friend loves mushrooms, so you decide to try something new and get both toppings!

   b. You both love the exact same topping (even when it's something wacky like pineapple!), so you get your favorite to share.

   c. You each want something completely different, so you decide to do half with your topping and half with hers.

2. You go back-to-school shopping and get an awesome new shirt. What is your friend's reaction?

   a. She loves it and wants to know when she can borrow it.

   b. She immediately goes out and buys the same one so you can match.

   c. She tells you it's not really her style, but she thinks it's perfect for you.

There's a Halloween party at school, and you and your best friend decide to come up with a costume together. What do you go as?

   a. One of you goes as milk and the other goes as a cookie.

   b. You go as Thing 1 and Thing 2 from Dr. Seuss's *The Cat in the Hat*.

   c. You can't agree on a costume so you each end up making your own instead.

In class, what are you and your best friend most likely to get in trouble for?

   a. Spending all of your time together and not including others

   b. Talking to each other

   c. Passing notes to each other

How long have you and your best friend known each other?

   a. Since birth! Your parents knew one another before you were even born, and you and your friend have been hanging out ever since.

   b. For a few years. You met at school or camp and instantly bonded over just how much you have in common.

   c. Only a few months. You just met this year, but it already feels like you've known each other all your lives.

6. It's your friend's birthday, and you want to get her the perfect gift. How do you decide what to get?

    a. You're with your friend so much that you already have 10 differen present ideas based on things she's talked about.

    b. You know she likes the same things as you, so you get her what you'd want to have for your own birthday.

    c. You have a little trouble deciding on just one idea so you get her a gift certificate to her favorite store so she can pick out her own present.

7. You decide to join the soccer team. What does your friend do when sh hears the news?

    a. She's already on the team—that's part of the reason you joined!

    b. She decides to play as well. What could be better than the two of you getting to spend more time together?

    c. She's excited for you and promises to make posters and come to every game to cheer you on.

8. How close do you and your best friend live to each other?

    a. Right next door or down the street

    b. In the neighborhood, just a short walk or bike ride away

    c. Across town, but you still see each other all the time

When people are talking about you and your best friend, they often remark:

    a. "They go together like peanut butter and jelly."

    b. "They're like two peas in a pod!"

    c. "Those two are like night and day."

. School's out and you have the whole summer ahead of you. How often will you see your best friend?

    a. Every. Single. Day.

    b. You're doing a lot of the same camps and activities so at least a few times a week.

    c. You don't always plan frequent hangouts, but when you do see each other you end up wanting to extend your time together and often have sleepovers.

. When you and your BFF listen to music together, what are you most likely to do?

    a. Learn all the words to a new song and create a choreographed dance routine

    b. You already have the same favorite song and play it on repeat

    c. Take turns picking songs and introducing each other to new music

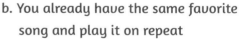

Your BFF Twins Score

Mostly A's = Attached at the hip

You and your best friend are practically inseperable! You spend so much time together that people are surprised when they see one of you alone. When you have a problem, your best friend is always nearby to offer advice or a helping hand. Although you never seem to get tired of each other, you make sure to find time to hang out with other friends as well.

Mostly B's = Identical twins

You and your best friend see a lot of each other because you have so many similar interests and hobbies! You rarely fight because you usually want to do the same things. Sometimes people even mistake you for each other or call you by your friend's name. Although you and your bestie usually agree on things, be sure to stay unique and true to yourself when you do have a different opinion.

Mostly C's = Separated at birth

You and your best friend are proof that opposites really do attract! Although you are very different from each other, the two of you have a special bond. Sometimes you even know what your bestie is going to say before she says it! Although you occasionally disagree on things, remember to remain calm, kind, and open-minded, and you just might be able to learn something new.

More This or That!

Get to know your BFF even better by sharing and comparing your answers to these This or That questions.

○ Sing or Dance? ○

○ Email or Snail Mail? ○

○ Cats or Dogs? ○

○ Books or Movies? ○

○ Snowmen or Sandcastles? ○

○ Sunrise or Sunset? ○

○ Roses or Tulips? ○

○ Gold or Silver? ○

○ Markers or Colored Pencils? ○

○ Ocean or Mountains? ○

○ Pencil or Pen? ○

○ Tag or Hide-and-Seek? ○

○ Skiing or Sledding? ○

○ Camping or Glamping? ○

○ Funny Movies or Scary Movies? ○

○ Thunderstorms or Snowstorms? ○

○ Wake Up Early or Sleep Late? ○

○ Travel by Car or Travel by Plane? ○

○ Soccer or Basketball? ○

○ Monopoly or Candy Land? ○

○ Summer or Fall? ○

Game Guide

Giggle all night long while getting to know your besties even better wit
these party games!

The Beach Ball Game

Buy an inflatable beach ball (the larger the better for big groups!) and
use permanent marker to write questions all over it. Once your ball is
covered with questions, have everyone make a circle and pick someone
to throw the ball to. The person who catches the ball will answer the
question that her right thumb is touching. After she answers the
question, she will throw the ball to another person whose turn it will
be to answer a question. Continue passing the ball until everyone has
had a turn to answer a few questions or until all the questions have
been answered!

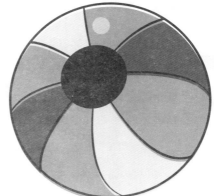

e Beach Ball Game Question Creator

me up with silly, soulful, and serious questions for your game ball.
k your guests to think of questions they might like to answer or hear
e answers to. Then have them each write down 3–5 questions or
oose from the list of questions below to get the game going!

Question Suggestions

What is your dream vacation?

If you could have any celebrity friend, who would it be?

Who is your favorite singer?

What was your last dream about?

What is one thing about you that no one knows?

What superpower would you like to have?

Truth or Dare

Truth or Dare is a game where one person asks a second person to pick "truth" or "dare." If the second person choos "truth," then the first person gets to ask her a question. If s chooses "dare" she must complete a task given to her. The person who completes the truth or the dare then asks a ne person to choose one, and she now gets to ask the question create the dare! Cut out the double-sided Truth or Dare card on the following pages or get creative and come up with y own questions. Then put the cards in a bowl and randomly pick one to be completed each time someone selects "truth" or "dare"!

Truth Cards

✂

Truth:
What's the weirdest thing you've ever eaten?

Truth:
What do you like the most about everyone in the room?

Truth:
Did you brush your teeth this morning?

Truth:
Are you afraid of the dark?

Truth:
Have you ever lied in Truth or Dare?

Truth:
What is your secret wish?

Dare Cards

Dare:
Try to lick your elbow while singing the alphabet.

Dare:
Dance crazy with no music on for 30 seconds.

Dare:
Have a 30-second conversation with your pillow.

Dare:
Act like a dog and fetch two objects.

Dare:
Try to scratch your armpit with your big toe.

Dare:
Wear your shirt backward for the rest of the game.

Truth:
Have you ever lied to a teacher?

Truth:
Do you sleep with a stuffed animal or special item?

Truth:
What was the best day of your life?

Truth:
What was the worst day of your life?

Truth:
If you could only take one thing to a deserted island,
what would you bring?

Truth:
Have you ever broken anything and
not told the person who it belonged to?

Dare Cards

Dare:
Hop on one leg for 30 seconds while flapping your arms like a bird.

Dare:
Let the person on your right give you any hairstyle she wants and then keep it that way for the rest of the game.

Dare:
Let someone put lipstick on you while she wears a blindfold.

Dare:
Keep a straight face for one minute while everyone tries to make you laugh.

Dare:
Exchange a clothing item with the person on your left.

Dare:
Do your best model runway walk around the room.